Understanding Oneself

Understanding Oneself

Adnan Khan

Copyright © 2021 by Adnan Khan
All rights reserved.

ISBN: 978-0-578-83082-7
eBook ISBN: 978-1-7364406-9-8

Cover design by Linh Hoang
Edited by Karin de Weille

www.explosionoflove.com

CONTENTS

What is Self-Understanding?	1
Insight into Movement of Thought	21
Explosion of Love	43

WHAT IS SELF-UNDERSTANDING?

Observing the world around us, from the clearly evident to the most subtle layers, we can see that our life is part of an extraordinarily complex web of physical and psychological relationships with all aspects of the cosmos. In order to engage in these relationships in the right way, it is absolutely essential that we understand ourselves. Without understanding ourselves, not only do we live in a perpetual state of inner confusion, but we also act as a source of disorder and chaos to the world at large. So how do we approach this delicate subject of self-understanding?

Before we begin our journey, we must ask ourselves sincerely if we comprehend the significance of understanding ourselves deeply. There must not be an ounce of doubt in our being that understanding oneself is of the greatest significance. If we do not yet comprehend the significance deeply, it is better to accept that we do not than to say that we comprehend it "intellectually." Dividing ourselves into intellectual, emotional, rational, irrational, and yet other parts is an act of introducing conflict in our being, because these "parts" come into tension with each other, naturally. Conflict expends our energy and keeps the mind occupied, such that we are never fully fresh to understand ourselves. On the other hand, if we comprehend the significance of understanding ourselves with our whole being, this very comprehension begins a journey of discovery of the ways of the self, a journey of immense insight and joy.

With deep clarity about the significance of understanding oneself, a question arises naturally: how must we understand ourselves? Throughout human existence, immense energy has been channeled into responding to this question. From the way the question is put forth, with its "how", it assumes that there is already a way out there that someone has figured out and to which we can adapt. Thus, we gravitate towards one of the many methods or systems which have infiltrated the world. These methods are put together by people with insight and wit, with promises grander than self-understanding, of freedom and salvation. But do they actually help us understand ourselves?

We have practiced these methods for hundreds or even thousands of years in the hope of finding our particular idea of freedom one day. That, of course, has not brought about the freedom we seek because we still suffer. We are held captive by our anxiety, fear, greed, hatred, envy, fear, and division. And we suffer from these movements in our being because we do not understand them. How can we understand them if we are chasing freedom all the time? Some may say that we suffer because we do not practice these methods completely, but that is just an excuse for the fact that these methods are only partial, for they are based on human knowledge, which is always partial. The advocates of these methods shy away from meeting the richness and vastness of reality, and fail to acknowledge that no method can account for the entire range of human experience. Therefore, in our inquiry, we let these methods be for a moment, and begin anew.

Now, instead of asking "how" can one understand oneself, what if we ask what does it mean to understand oneself? Let us pause for a moment and ask ourselves: what does it mean to understand myself? Putting the question this way opens up an opportunity for us to inquire into the question together, so that if one comprehends what it means to understand oneself, one can go on to understand oneself without needing to follow the prescriptions of a method created by someone else. Instead of following yet another complex method to achieve freedom, can we not claim our freedom right at the outset? For surely, without freedom, we can never really inquire, we can only follow. Therefore, freedom must be at the beginning of the inquiry, not at the end, so that we can inquire freely into our own being instead of chasing a mere image of freedom.

Since we are inquiring into this matter together, let us make sure that we are not reading passively, but are inquiring actively, full of energy, resolved to find out for ourselves what it means to understand oneself, actually. Perhaps we can use the words in this book as nothing more than a mirror to observe what is going on in our own being. If we can observe our being in the light of these words, we have already begun our inquiry. Without such a state of being, what we are reading may be yet another "idea" or a "concept" with little grounding in the reality of our own lives, thus moving us away from ourselves instead of bringing us home to that which is moving within us. So, let us come home together, to ourselves, as we read on.

So, what does it mean to understand oneself? Or putting it more simply, what is self-understanding? We may respond to this question with what we have come to understand about ourselves, like, I am this kind of a person, I like these kinds of things, or this is my purpose in life etc. While all of these may be true, is that what it means to understand oneself? Does it allow us to understand what may arise in our being right now? Or, is this self-understanding merely a set of conclusions and memories, based on our experience of course, but entirely of the past, carried over by thought into the present, and projected into the future?

Let us assume that self-understanding really

is this set of static conclusions and memories. Then, can we find out if this helps us understand ourselves in this moment right now? Suppose a feeling arises freshly in the moment - take what you are feeling right now - how do we make sense of the feeling from the perspective that we already understand ourselves? If we feel that we have already understood ourselves, instead of observing how the feeling unravels, unknowingly we begin to relate the present feeling to a feeling we may have felt in the past. We may recount from memory what that feeling may have been - suppose fear - and all of a sudden, onto a feeling that was totally fresh, all that was associated with fear creeps into our being. Our being begins to tremble. We try to escape this fear, yet the onslaught of feelings has just begun. Sorrow, loneliness, guilt, separation, and shame cascade through our being. We continue to react to the feeling with justifications about why we are feeling this way, followed by judgements that we should not feel this way. We think thoughts to soothe ourselves, and try to distract ourselves from what we are feeling. If one of these thoughts or distractions finally works, the feeling is shoved back into the abyss from where it arose, only to leave a lingering fear behind that it may arise yet again. Thus, fear continues to operate in our being, unresolved, never understood.

We are seeing that not only is our past understanding always governing our experience in the present moment, but to combat the fear that the feeling may return, this understanding is projected into the future. Is this what it means to understand oneself, a constant process of perpetuating the past into the present and the future? If the future is a forward projection of our past, is it not merely a repetition of the past, modified ever so slightly? Can we pause for a moment and look within, to observe without judgement, if this is how we function?

Through this typical situation, we are discovering something quite profound about ourselves: the past with its conclusions and memories, that which we may call self-understanding, deeply affects our thoughts and feelings in the present moment. We are not saying that this is wrong or right: all we are doing is understanding clearly that this may be the case, without judgement. If this is what is going on inside us most of the time, can we ever fully understand something that is arising freshly in the moment? Clearly not! If our mind is so deeply occupied with these static conclusions and memories about itself, it does not have the capacity to look at what is alive and arising in the present moment without the burden of the past. If we recognize what is arising as fear, but try to escape it based on a past pattern, we never understand fear, and hence can never go beyond it.

Again, we note that we are not saying that we must drop the past, we are just discovering how we actually function. We are discovering what *is*.

Now, suppose if we find ourselves in front of a flower that is beginning to bloom. What do we do? Do we take our eyes off this astonishing affair? Of course not! We stare at the flower without a thought, completely awestruck, with our eyes wide open, observing every movement of the flower as it unfurls. That is what it means to *observe*.

We have all experienced a state of presence like this in one way or another. A moment later we may say "how beautiful!" But that is a conclusion, brought about by the movement of thought. If we continue to fixate on the thought of the beautiful flower, we stop observing the flower, which is still right in front of us, unraveling eternal beauty in our presence. This is how the movement of thought brings the past into the present. As we go on with our day thinking about how much pleasure the flower has brought us and is going to bring us, the movement of thought projects the past into the future.

Similarly, as a feeling arises in the present moment, is it too not like a blooming flower, in that it is completely fresh and alive, without a name? So the question is, can we observe this feeling with our complete being, just like we observed the blooming flower, with curiosity and awe, without judgement, attending to every movement of what *is*? Say we notice a feeling arise, and notice that our being recognizes it as fear. We can observe this tendency of our being to name and label feelings. The feeling may invoke pain, we may feel like running away from it, but we can observe this tendency to escape, too. We may be seized with fear of being stuck with this feeling forever, but we can observe this intensity of feeling, too. The feeling may last a few minutes or a few hours, but as we observe every movement of the feeling, we begin to understand ourselves as we are: we begin to discover the ways of the self, what is actually going on in our being, that which has no name. In this attention there is no fear. Not attending to the fact, and the very effort to escape the fact is fear.

Thus, in order to understand what *is*, we must *observe* what *is*, which includes the movement of thought as well as the movement of memories of the past, and hopes for the future. So, what we are discovering together is that self-understanding is not a static set of conclusions about oneself that one carries about. Self-understanding is an action only of the present moment: it is the act of observing oneself as one *is*, in *this* moment right now, *always*. And since what is going on inside us is not static, but always changing, awareness has to be swift in observation. This awareness must be alert, full of energy - like a stream flowing down a valley - but effortless and passive, because effort expends energy. One may feel the desire to sustain this clear awareness into the next moment, the future - as we do, when we find a moment of peace or relief from anxiety - but that again is a movement of thought, a desire. A swift awareness can observe and understand the tendency that our thoughts are always in movement between the future and the past. Thus, observation deepens our insight into the ways of the self, one moment at a time.

Please note that we have said nothing of the kind that we ought to "live in the present moment." We often carry such proclamations, images, and ideas around in our mind, but we can see now that they burden our mind, and distract us from observing what *is*. They also accentuate our tendency to judge ourselves when we are not acting in accord with them. What we are understanding together is that we are interested in a complete understanding of our being, for which we must observe all that arises in us, including the memories of the past, fantasies of the future, basically, each and every movement of our being.

Whether or not we understand ourselves in

the way we have just discovered, we can all attest to the fact that we are deeply conditioned by our past, which includes both our personal lives, and the millions of years of evolution. This conditioning, interacting with the current state of the world, brings us very little joy, for we are eternally spinning in and out of deep states of anxiety, loneliness, envy, greed, hate, and separateness, etc. These tendencies give rise to an immense degree of disorder in our being, such that we have no relationship with ourselves, and as a result, no relationship with other humans, animals and the environment. Because we do not understand the depths of these conflicts, they perpetuate forward in time, unresolved, entangling ever more deeply with each other, leading to intense states of disorder in our actions. So, the eternal question is: do we take the consequences of our conditioning as necessary, arguing that our conflicts are unsolvable and live with them, or can we do something about it?

This is why we inquired together into what it means to understand oneself. As we observe all that arises in our being moment after moment, with lucidity and vitality, we begin to discover the ways of the self with clarity. As we observe a feeling we may have previously called fear, we discover that it is actually an interesting phenomenon with a life of its own every time it arises. Though it may be dark and heavy, its texture has a sense of freshness, for it is never quite the same as the previous time. Discovering this, we begin to observe fear ever more carefully (which means full of care) as it reveals its story more clearly, more innocently, more gracefully.

The immensity of existence can still

overwhelm the mind, and arouse a great sense of confusion and disorder in our being. Unless we begin to understand this confusion and disorder without trying to end it, a fundamental transformation is impossible. The insights arising from observing and understanding the inner confusion and disorder are what transform us, just as understanding something confusing transforms our discomfort into ease. Therefore, *observation* is *understanding*, and *understanding* is *transformation*. This transformation is the beginning of order.

Not only is this transformation personal, it is also societal, because we are society and society is composed of us. In becoming aware of how our tendencies affect our actions, we begin to see others as we see ourselves, all acting from similar conditioning. In this way, we suddenly find ourselves in the universal realm of humanity: while the particular contents and intensities of our feelings may be different from those of others, the basic texture of our feelings is almost the same, for after all, we are the same organism. Thus, each one of us resolving conflicts in our being with such a voracious appetite, begins to bring a great sense of order to our actions, hence bringing a fundamental sense of order to society.

Finally, we note that we are not speaking of a practice or an exercise we must engage in periodically so that one day, we can resolve our conflicts, relieve our suffering, and achieve freedom! Isn't that what a method wants us to believe? What we have come to understand together is that conflict in our being is brought to an end by observing and understanding it *as* it arises. Thus, by *observing*, we remain in a perpetual state of *transformation*, always claiming our freedom in the moment at hand.

INSIGHT INTO MOVEMENT OF THOUGHT

Together, we have come to understand that understanding oneself means to observe oneself as one *is*, in the moment at hand. Any psychological insight or image about oneself, carried over to the next moment, is merely memory, and a mind burdened with memory cannot observe and understand that which *is*. Memories, conclusions, and intentions are ideas about reality. Reality and truth, on the other hand, are always waiting to be discovered freshly in the *present* moment.

A natural question then arises: what does one understand about oneself as one begins to observe oneself in the moment at hand? While the particulars may vary depending on what our minds are preoccupied with, we begin to see that we are always consumed by thought. From the moment we wake up to the moment we go to bed, and possibly while we are sleeping, we are thinking. This means that most of the energy of our being is expended in thinking. Once again, we note that we have no intention to proclaim this as right or wrong, for we are just observing how we function.

As we find out that we are perpetually consumed by thought, we become curious about this ever-changing, ever-flowing movement in our mind, which we will call the *movement of thought* from here on. Now what do we find out when we observe this movement more carefully? What do you observe about your thoughts as you sit here and stare into empty space for a moment?

Are most of our thoughts not self-concerning? About my life, my problems, my goals, my progress, my ambitions, my fears, my desires, my fulfillment? Does this not make us feel incredibly lonely, as if there is a vast chasm between us and everything else? We may judge ourselves at first when we see that we are so self-consumed. However, since we have already come to appreciate the power of observing ourselves without judgement, we continue to observe this judgement without further judgement. For we have realized that judgement is nothing but a reaction to what *is*, and reaction - which may lead to yet another reaction - hinders us from observing and understanding what *is*.

Now, given that almost the entire energy of our being is consumed by the movement of thought, is it not important to ask if thinking occupies the right place in our lives? In other words, are we in the right relationship with thinking? Is this merely an "intellectual" question, or does it actually have relevance to our daily lives? Let us discover together why it is important.

Firstly, if the relentless movement of self-concerning thought fatigues and tires out our mind, can we meet the richness of life with freshness and vitality? Clearly not. Secondly, if at times, we actually need to think deeply about a challenging situation, a real problem, will we have the energy to approach the problem with an open and vigorous mind if we are fixated on our own problems? Most likely not. With half-butchered thinking, we may patch up a "solution" to the problem, but we do this at the expense of internal peace, aware of the fact that we did not do our best. Does it not make sense then to inquire into the question of what the right place of thinking in life is, so that this powerful aspect of our being can be engaged in the right way, to end our internal conflict instead of perpetuating it forward?

Our mind may have already begun thinking about the question, but we must pause here, and ask: since the very question is about our relationship with thinking, is thinking the right way to approach the question? Furthermore, given that our mind may already be fatigued from the movement of self-concerning thought, can we even tackle a problem as deep as this? So, how do we approach this matter completely differently?

Since the question concerns thinking, can we ask ourselves if we completely understand the movement of thought? As of yet, the answer is no. Each one of us can observe in ourselves that thought brings both order and disorder in our mind, and because we do not understand the movement of thought deeply enough, we try to bring order with more self-concerned thinking. Some of us may be shaking our heads frantically in disagreement, arguing, that actually, not thinking enough may be the cause of the disorder. We agree with that sentiment, but only partially. Let us see why.

Thought can indeed bring some order to our mind, but because we do not understand the entire movement of thought, this order is only partial: it breaks down the moment thoughts get out of control. And hell breaks loose. We do not have to look far to see the truth of this fact. Just consider the state of your mind when you find yourself in a bout of anxiety or cannot fall asleep one night: no thought can end the onslaught of thoughts, regardless of how reasonable it may be. This shows that we do not understand the movement of thought completely, and therefore cannot control it with more thought.

So, how can we begin to understand the entire movement of thought? We discovered in the last chapter that in order to understand what *is*, we must *observe* what *is*, without judgement. So, can we begin to observe the movement of thought as it moves in our being? Now, what is it that we begin to understand as we *observe* each and every movement of thought? Try it for yourself, even if for a moment.

We begin to see how thoughts arise and fade, how one thought leads to a cascade of other thoughts, how thoughts excite us, how they arouse desire and fear. We see how we are so deeply consumed by the contents of our thoughts, that we often perceive them to be reality. As we observe the entire movement of thought yet more deeply, we notice that our mind is also infiltrated with images, of ourselves and others, acting as seeds to the trees of thought. We are aware of the fact that we often make an effort to conform to an image, either one that we have of ourselves or one that others have of us. But do we understand the consequence of trying to conform to an image?

In trying to conform to an image, our mind remains occupied by the image, always thinking of ways to turn the image into reality. Since our attention remains so deeply occupied, we never come to understand ourselves and others as we actually *are*, hence destroying our relationship with ourselves and others. We may be in conversation with a friend, but in reality, we may only be interacting with an image we have of them in our mind. We may be looking at ourselves in a mirror, but only through the narrow lens of our own thoughts and images. Now, can we observe in our own being that this may be the case? Can we observe the movement of thought to observe how these images influence us, and see if we can understand ourselves and others, actually? Let us go deeper into the movement of thought.

Suppose we come across a flower. First there is perception, sensation, or observation of the flower. Based on this perception or memory, thought comes into movement, and we say, 'a rose!' Can we see that before thought begins to move, there is only observation, without a separation of "I" as the observer of "the rose." But as soon as thought comes into movement, there arises a feeling in us that we are the observer, the perceiver, the experiencer of what is observed, the rose; hence a separation arises between the observer and the observed. Without thought, there is no observer, there is only observation. It is the movement of thought that brings about the feeling that there is an observer, "me." Thus, the feeling of being "me," is a part of the movement of thought, not apart from it.

Let us slow down yet more. When thinking, we usually have a feeling that "I" am the "thinker" of "thoughts," do we not? Suppose a thought arouses fear. Does the thinker in us not separate itself from the thought, so it can suppress the thought in the hope of protecting itself from fear? Unknowingly, we are functioning like this all the time. The relentless movement of thought is always engaged in dividing the mind between the "thinker" and "thought." The thinker, which is a part of the movement of thought - as we found out earlier - acts on thought as if it is apart from it, to gain a sense of control and security. As a consequence, thought elevates the status of the thinker to higher and higher levels. The thinker becomes such a dominant feature of thought, that the mind cannot perceive the fact anymore, that the thinker is a part of the movement of thought, not apart from it.

Let us pause here for a moment. Are we beginning to understand that our mind is operating under the illusion that the "thinker" is separate from "thought?" Can we ask this of ourselves: am I, the thinker, separate or independent from the movement of thought? When observing oneself, is the observer not the observed? See if you can find out for yourself.

Once we fully understand that the thinker in us is not separate from the movement of thought - by seeing it in ourselves, not because it is asserted by someone else - the illusion of separation between the "thinker" and "thought" begins to come to an end, and one begins to see for oneself that inwardly there is no separation between the observer and the observed, that the observer is the observed. Then there is just observation of the entire movement of thought, without the thinker making an effort to control thought.

Before we see what this entails, let us see if we can visualize through metaphor how the thinker is a part of the movement of thought: is the ocean separate from the waves? No, the ocean is the waves! Is the blooming of a flower separate from the flower? No, the blooming is the flower. Concerning feelings and emotions: when we feel angry, are we not anger? When we feel greedy, are we not greed? When we feel joyful, are we not joy? Similarly, when we are thinking, we are the movement of thought.

Now, what does this discovery of the thinker being a part of the movement of thought have to do with understanding ourselves? It has everything to do with it! Let us see how: when a thought arises, we try to hold onto it if it is pleasurable, and try to get rid of it if it is painful by thinking other thoughts. Sometimes this can relieve anxiety, but at other times, the onslaught of thoughts takes us deeper into darkness as we continue to combat thoughts with more thoughts. Thus, the energy of our being is constantly squandered in one part of our mind, the thinker, trying to control another part, the thought, an action founded on the confusion that the thinker is separate from thought and can therefore control it. But as we have discovered, there is no separation between the thinker and thought.

When we react to one thought with another, without noticing that we are reacting, not only do we lose the possibility of understanding why we reacted the way we did, we also fail to understand how the thought made us feel in that moment. Hence, we never understand the intricacies of thought. If we fully understand that the thinker is part of the movement of thought, we begin to understand that there is no "me" separate from the thought who can act on the thought to control it. Thus, we begin to observe thoughts as they flower and wither, one after another, understanding the entire movement of thinking.

As a concrete example, let us consider a

movement of mind we call fear. Physical fear arises when we are in a life-threatening situation. It prompts us to take the appropriate action to bring that fear to an end. However, what we want to explore is psychological fear. This fear is a state of mind, without a threat to our life but a threat to our psychological comfort and security. For example, fear of loneliness, fear that we may not be making the best of our life, that we may never be free of our struggles, are all psychological fears. However, because we react to psychological fear just like we react to physical fear, by trying to escape it, we never quite understand its subtleties. As we begin to observe the movement of our thoughts in a state of fear, fear begins to reveal its story. We begin to see that psychological fear cannot be understood without also understanding desire, for fear often arises from the thought that our desire may not be fulfilled: fear of loneliness is inseparable from the desire for companionship. So, desire and fear are two sides of the same coin.

Now, what is it that brings desire and fear into motion? Suppose we come across the idea of a marvelous spiritual experience, or more simply, a beautiful person. First there is observation, perception, sensation. Soon thought comes into movement, giving rise to the thinker, the "me," as separate from the experience or the person. The thinker, separated by thought into "me," dominates the movement of thought, and begins to desire the experience or the person. Very soon, fear arises because of the thought that our desire may not be fulfilled. Thus, fear and desire are brought into motion by the movement of self-concerning thought.

It is important to understand the deep inter-relationship between desire and fear without making an effort to end them, because the very effort to end them is the movement of yet another desire, of a more subtle kind, disguised as spiritual transcendence or self-improvement. This desire to achieve a higher state of being occupies one's attention, making one think of ways to achieve that state. This self-concerned thinking hinders the mind from observing and understanding the movement of desire and fear, and therefore, it is unable to go beyond them.

Understanding that thought is not only the source of psychological fear, but also the source of desire - which can also manifest as ambition, greed, and envy - is a tremendous breakthrough. For it means that the mind has become aware that its very own movement is the source of its confusion and suffering. This is the beginning of a fundamental transformation, of a nature completely different from the change we desire to bring about by acting on our own thoughts with more thoughts. The thinker, acting on thought, of course causes a change. However, this change is always partial, solving one problem while giving rise to another, a natural consequence of a divided mind. Such a divided mind can never transform fundamentally. Therefore, the entire movement of thought must be understood.

As the observation of the entire movement of thought continues with such care and attention, without judgement, non-verbally, this relentless movement begins to slow down. Then, what arises surprisingly, and most naturally, is silence. This silence is not brought about by self-hypnotizing techniques - of what many may call "meditation" - with the goal of disciplining the mind into yet another habit, albeit silence. This silence has arisen completely naturally from the mind turning inwards and understanding its own movements with freedom, without a prescription, without a method. This understanding is the true meaning of meditation. To understand oneself, one can sit by oneself and observe what is moving within, or one can observe oneself in a room full of people to see how one manifests in relationships with others. Any form of discipline that replaces old habits of the mind with new habits, however "noble" and "virtuous," is not meditation. Habits constrain the mind and make it dull. They create resistance in ones being to understanding what *is*, and a mind in resistance can never inquire and understand freely. Understanding has an inward discipline of its own, completely self-sustaining.

In silence, the mind begins to see clearly all the movements within and without. It discovers the deep inter-relationship of the outer world with the inner, coming into a completely new relationship with everything it interacts with, a relationship in which the separation between the inside and the outside dissolves. The mind listens to another silently, observing all the movements in itself and the other without a boundary between the two. It looks at a mountain, a flower, a bird, a face, or a sunset without grasping for words, quietly. The mind stops grasping for experience and begins to rest in what *is*. Resting in this deeply sensitive state, the mind thinks with freshness when it encounters a problem. And when it does not need to think, it rests without being consumed by self-concerning thought.

We must note here, that self-concern should not be confused with self-care. Self-care is the act of tending to whatever needs care - say a wound - as well as tending to all that is going on within. On the other hand, self-concern is the perpetual movement of thought about oneself, as if one is the center of the cosmos. This is the source of our loneliness, a feeling of absolute disconnection from the world: for when we feel we are the center, all our actions are self-centered, such that our relationships are not relationships actually, but merely self-serving affairs. However, when self-concerning thought comes to an end, there is no "thinker" anymore, and hence no center: the dissolution of this center brings one into the right relationship with all aspects of the cosmos because a mental boundary between the inside and outside has ceased to exist, thus ending one's loneliness.

The ending of self-concerning thought is not a state that can be perpetuated forward in time once it arises. It is only alive as one observes all movements of the mind carefully, but effortlessly, in the present moment. Thus, past and future states of mind are irrelevant to such a being. Of course, we must plan the future science experiment and the steps to fight a disease, but we can only do this with greatest vitality if our minds are not fatigued with self-concerning thought. Hence, thinking naturally finds the right place in life with the ending of self-concerning thought, a natural consequence of observing and understanding oneself.

EXPLOSION OF LOVE

Together, we have discovered that when the movement of self-concerning thought comes to an end in the present moment, silence arises naturally, full of energy that was previously expended in the effort to control thought. A natural question then arises: what is the place of this immense energy, inherent in silence, in our daily life? We must ask this question in order to bring silence down from the pedestal and the ravings of spiritualists, and see for ourselves how it may actually manifest in our personal lives. If we do not ask this question, then silence is yet another idea or image amongst the many that infiltrate our mind, and all we have come to understand thus far, is merely a mentally stimulating adventure, with no grounding in reality. So let us find out together how the energy in silence manifests in our daily life.

We are asking a question akin to what physicists ask when they are exploring different forms of energy. They ask, for example, how does the immense energy in a star manifest? We discover that it manifests in many forms ranging from visible-light to heat to gravity. Similarly, we can ask, how does the energy inherent in silence manifest psychologically? Of course, we use the physicists' exploration only as a metaphor, for unlike light or gravity, it is not quite evident how the psychological energy manifests. So, how do we approach this question?

Perhaps we can get a visceral feel of the energy inherent in silence by revisiting briefly, how silence arose in the first place. We began our inquiry with what it means to understand oneself - and found out together - that, in order to understand oneself, one must observe oneself as one is at all times - carefully but without effort. Observing ourselves revealed that we are perpetually consumed by self-concerning thought. By observing the movement of thought, we came to understand that it is thought that gives rise to a feeling that there is a thinker "me", separate from thought. In reality, however, the thinker is a part of the movement of thought, but because it feels as if it is separate, it tries to control thoughts with more thoughts. This illusion of separation between "me" and "my thoughts" hinders us from understanding the movement of thought.

When we understand fully, that in reality, there is no separation between the thinker and thought, we begin to observe the movement of thought instead of trying to control it. Thus, the energy previously expended in self-concerning thought, is channeled into careful observation of the movements of the mind. It is this state of perpetual observation in which silence flowers into being, completely naturally. This silence, born of understanding, is not dull but highly active, alert, sensitive, and full of potential.

In such a deep state of observation, one is always discovering and understanding the ways of the self and the ways of the world. One is incredibly sensitive to all that is happening inside and outside. Therefore, one can respond most appropriately to what the moment demands: if it demands one to think, one can think with full energy, for one is not fatigued with the relentless movement of thought. Thus, a deep intelligence within has awakened.

A being in such a deep state of observation and understanding is sensitive to both joy and sorrow, and can therefore feel intense compassion towards all aspects of existence. Self-concern no longer prevents the being from feeling one with that which is in pain or in need of support. Thus, one helps and supports those in need not in order to feel happy or fulfilled - which is merely self-concern - but because it is the right thing to do. One does not need to be motivated by ideas of virtue and salvation because intelligence and compassion are a natural consequence of understanding.

A being so sensitive, intelligent, and compassionate does not project its desires outwardly or even inwardly, because it understands that the desire to change itself or another is a hindrance to understanding what *is*. Understanding is itself a transformation. Trying to change oneself or others without understanding what *is*, is an act of violence, for in the effort to conform oneself or another to an image, regardless of how noble, virtuous, or holy it may be, one gives rise to conflict between what *is* and what *should be*. Such conflict is the source of chaos in our being and our relationships.

The intelligence arising from understanding guides one to continue to attend to what *is*, instead of trying to change it. Such tending is the true nature of love, in that it is an action free from thought, conditions, and desires. Being in love with something means one is deeply attending to it. So, to attend to something is the action of love. Even in a moment of anger or fear, attending to what is going on within, is an act of love.

Attention is the very state in which we are transformed, naturally. It is the fertile ground in which love has exploded in one's being, bringing immense joy. Because this love is not born of attachment, but complete understanding, there is complete freedom. At the same time, one is completely vulnerable - like a flower that can be swept off by the wind - for love has opened the gates for the entire spectrum of human experience to sweep through one's being.

A being so sensitive, intelligent, compassionate, exploding with love and joy, is in a perpetual state of transformation. One is always learning wholly, not partially as one does when one is awfully clever in a particular thing, say finance or physics. Such partial wit is a means of self-fulfillment and self-stimulation, and is merely a self-concerning activity. Attachment to a self-concerning activity imprisons one within a tight compartment of life, such that one remains psychologically impoverished, unable to come into relationship with the greater movement of life. Thus, cleverness and wit without sensitivity, compassion, and love is not at all intelligence but mere perpetuation of partial activity, which adds to the already abundant disorder, and shifts life away from wholeness.

Let us take a moment to check ourselves to make sure that we are not intellectualizing about some abstract ideas of love. We are simply pointing to the love born of observation, understanding, sensitivity, and compassion. This love is an engagement of all faculties of our being, akin to the state when a mother sees her child in pain: there is no intellectualizing, she just acts, however it may be. So love is action. Thought of love is not love, it is merely thought. The love we have discovered guides the powerful instrument of thought to its right place in life. With love, we continue to understand ourselves and all others in the present moment. Amidst the chaos of life, this is the beginning of order in our being and our relationships, an order that is a source of a fundamental transformation of the world.

This transformation is only evident when we see it. We cannot foresee it, for we have been immersed in self-concern so deeply that it is very difficult for us to imagine the outcome of the love we have discovered together. This love awaits discovery in our being and the world in every moment. The wonderful news is that we have already begun this journey, and can sail onwards as we look at a tree silently, listening to the wind sifting through its leaves, smelling the fragrance of its bark, touching the life that throbs in its trunk, and tasting the essence of the cosmos in its *entirety*, one moment at a time, moment by moment, in every moment, including this moment.

GRATITUDE AND SUPPORT

Thank you for sharing this journey with us. We are committed to making this book more easily available to readers, financially. If the book has touched your heart in any way, and you would like to support us in making it more widely available, please visit: www.explosionoflove.com

www.ingramcontent.com/pod-product-compliance
Lightning Source LLC
Chambersburg PA
CBHW022000290426
44108CB00012B/1145